C000112433

HOW TO GET

RICH

Jeff Fisher

BLOOMSBURY

FOR INFORMATION ADDRESS
BLOOMSBURY, 175 FIFTH AVENUE,
NEW YORK, N.Y. 10010
PUBLISHED BY BLOOMSBURY
NEW YORK AND LONDON
DISTRIBUTED TO THE TRADE BY
HOLTZBRINCK PUBLISHERS
CATALOGING-IN-PUBLICATION
DATA IS AVAILABLE FROM
THE LIBRARY OF CONGRESS
ISBN 1-58234-270-9
FIRST U.S. EDITION 2002
10 9 8 7 6 5 4 3 2 1
PRINTED IN GREAT BRITAIN
BY ST. EDMUNDSBURY PRESS,
SUFFOLK

YOU START OUT
WITH NOTHING

YOU ATTEMPT A
MODEST LIVING
BY HARD WORK,
DECENCY, FRUGALITY,
AND INTEGRITY

YOU SCRUB THE
POOP DECK

YOU PAINT THE TROUSERS
ONTO AN ENDLESS LINE
OF PORCELAIN FIGURES

YOU HANDSTITCH
TINY PARTS OF
PIECES OF RUBBISH
TO OTHER BITS

YOU OFFICE

YOU PUSH YOURSELF
BEYOND THE LIMITS
OF HUMAN ENDURANCE

YOU REALIZE
YOUR MISTAKE

YOU CONSTRUCT AN
ELABORATE PERSONA,
INVOLVING DUTCH
ROYALTY, VINTAGE
CARS AND ADOPTED
MANNERISMS, PURELY
FROM FOUND OBJECTS

YOU MEAN TO MARRY
THE TREMENDOUSLY RICH
LADY KLIPPLOCH OF
MUDDERSCKHLASSEN

YOU CHARM, YOU
POLO TILL DAWN

HER FATHER, LORD
FOOTSTOOL, SETS
THE DOGS ON YOU

YOU WIN
£1,000,000,000,000,000.00

YOU SPEND IT

YOU EXPLOIT A
DEFENCELESS MINORITY

YOU ARE LYNCHED AND
BURNT IN THE STREET

YOU PAINT YOUR
MASTERPIECE

NO-ONE
WANTS IT

YOU GO INTO
INSURANCE

AN ENDLESS
STRING OF NATURAL
DISASTERS AND
MISPLACED DOUBLE
BUY-BACKS APPEARS
UNEXPECTEDLY
AT YOUR DOOR. YOU
CAN'T REMEMBER
WHY IT WAS, WHERE
YOU PUT IT, OR WHO THE HEL

YOU LOSE
THE PLOT

YOU OWE $1,000,000,
000,000,000,000,000,
000,000,000,000,000,
000,000,000,000,000,
000,000,000,000,000

YOU MAKE A
RUN FOR IT

YOU LUNCH

YOU ANNEX A TINY
FOREIGN ENCLAVE

YOU PILLAGE,
YOU PLUNDER

YOU CHANGE
YOUR IDENTITY

YOU FIND £1,000,
000,000,000,000,
000,000,000,000,
000,000,000,000,
000,000,000,000

YOU LIVE
LIKE A KING

YOU'RE ROBBED
AT KNIFEPOINT

YOU ATTEMPT
SELLING YOUR BODY

YOU GAMBLE

YOU SELL
YOUR MOTHER

YOU BECOME AN
APOLOGIST FOR
SOME APPALLING
FORM OF TOXIC WASTE

YOU SLEEP WITH
YOUR BOSS

YOU INVEST
IN ART

YOU WIN AT
THE TRACK

YOU BUY
PIG FUTURES

MALE 48
REQUIRES VAST
PERSONAL WEALTH
WILL DO ANYTHING
GBC. GIRLY. YLPAT.
HYLW. 164311226

YOU ADVERTISE

YOU LITIGATE

YOU EXTRACT

YOU LOSE IT

YOUR BANK ROBS
YOU AT KNIFEPOINT

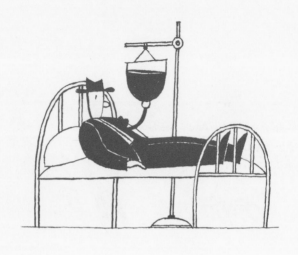

YOU ARE TAXED
MERCILESSLY

YOU INVENT AN
INDISPENSABLE GADGET

YOUR BOAT
COMES IN

YOUR BOAT
GOES OUT

YOUR DEBT TO SOCIETY
PAID, YOU RETIRE TO A LIFE
OF CONTEMPLATION

INCREDIBLY ENOUGH,
BENEATH THE POTATOES,
YOU CHANCE UPON THE LOST
TOMB OF ZIB THE GOLDEN

A MULTITUDE OF
SMALL CREATURES CARRIES
YOU OFF TO THE LAND
BEYOND THE CLOUDS WHERE
YOU ARE DECLARED
KING OF HEAVEN,
FED FRESH FISH,
CHOCOLATE CAKE &
AS MUCH WINE AS
YOU CAN DRINK......

EVERYTHING GOES BLACK